Christian Perspe
on
Development Is

Series Editor: Enda McDonagh

HUMAN RIGHTS

Linda Hogan

TRÓCAIRE *VERITAS* **CAFOD** SCIAF

TRÓCAIRE

Catholic Agency for World Development,
Maynooth,
Co. Kildare,
Ireland.

Tel: +353 1 629 3333
Fax: +353 1 629 0661
e-mail: info@trocaire.ie
http://www.trocaire.org

VERITAS

Veritas House,
7-8 Lr Abbey Street,
Dublin 1,
Ireland.

Tel: +353 1 878 8177
Fax: +353 1 878 6507
http://www.veritas.ie

C⁷AFOD

Catholic Fund for Overseas Development,
Romero Close,
Stockwell Road,
London SW9 8TY,
U.K.

Tel: +44 171 733 7900
Fax: +44 171 274 9630
e-mail: hqcafod@cafod.org.uk
http://www.cafod.org.uk

SCIAF

5, Oswald Street,
Glasgow G1 4QR.

Tel: 0141 - 2214447

© 2nd edition 2002
   Linda Hogan

Design/layout: Harrison Design
Printed in Ireland by Genprint

ISBN 1 85390 496 1

Contents

Foreword
Bishop John Kirby, Chairman of Trócaire

Anniversaries are a time for looking back and reviewing what we have accomplished and what remains undone, as well as for looking forward, renewing commitment and rededicating ourselves to the task. On the occasion of Trócaire's 25th anniversary in 1998, we reviewed various aspects of our work overseas and at home.

A major international conference explored the issue of People, Power and Participation and considered civil society in the developing world and its role in protecting, preserving and promoting human rights and democracy. Ten eminent human rights defenders with whom Trócaire has worked in the three continents of the South spoke eloquently of the denial of the most basic rights to millions of the world's citizens. Speakers echoed the words of Pope John Paul II when he said that "A type of development which does not respect and promote human rights is not really worthy of humankind" (*Sollicitudo Rei Socialis, 33*).

The founding documents of Trócaire gave the organisation a very clear mandate and situated this within the work of the Church and within Catholic Social Teaching. The anniversary year provided an opportunity to focus anew on the Christian inspiration behind the work of Trócaire.

This led to the decision to produce a joint Trócaire/Veritas series exploring Christian perspectives on key development issues. We are delighted to have our sister development agencies in the UK, CAFOD and SCIAF, as co-publishers of the series. We have invited eminent scholars to examine major strands in the work of our agencies and to elucidate from a theological perspective the impulses that motivate the practical projects and programmes which Trócaire, CAFOD and SCIAF support around the developing world. The result is a rich resource of analysis, reflection and restatement of the Christian commitment to solidarity and the oneness of the human family.

I would like to pay tribute to each of the authors for contributing so generously of their talent and their time in the preparation of these Reflections. We owe to our series editor, Professor Enda McDonagh, a profound gratitude for the inspiring guidance he has shown to authors and Trócaire staff engaged in this project. The output is of great practical use to Trócaire, CAFOD and SCIAF in charting their way as well as being of interest to all of those concerned to rise to the challenge of creating a world suffused by the Christian commitment to the dignity of each and every person.

INTRODUCTION
Enda McDonagh, Series Editor

As part of the celebrations of the 25th anniversary of its foundation and more importantly in preparation for its work in the new millennium, Trócaire began a fresh examination of its Christian-Catholic roots. With the help of an inter-disciplinary group of advisors and with Veritas, Cafod and SCIAF as co-publishers it has initiated a series of brief, accessible studies under the general title "Christian Perspectives on Development Issues". The aim of these studies is to set in dialogue the rich and varied Christian tradition in teaching and practice of commitment to the poor and excluded with the current concerns of development agencies like Trócaire, Cafod and SCIAF. In this way it is hoped to enlighten the Christian understanding and renew the spiritual energies of these three agencies and their staff at home and abroad, and of their supporters and contributors. Without such enlightenment and renewal the vision and work of these agencies could become narrow and frustrating.

To ensure that such studies are really helpful the particular topics must be carefully chosen in the light of people's needs and our agencies commitments. The first titles in the series, *Human Rights*, *Land* and *Famine* illustrate three of the most urgent concerns for Trócaire, Cafod and SCIAF and other development agencies. In seeking to expose Christian perspectives on these issues, the authors have undertaken a practical theological exploration from biblical background to contemporary analysis. While maintaining close communication with concrete problems of the day they have drawn on developing Christian tradition to illuminate and deepen commitment to justice in the world, that commitment element of the Gospel as the 1971 Synod of Bishops called it.

The series is designed not only to enhance the understanding and motivation of development agencies and workers; the studies themselves make clear how much theology has to learn from work in the field, how much theory has to gain from praxis. In fact the socio encyclicals which form the basis of so much social thought and activity in the Church were themselves influenced at various times by practical developments as individual Church people and organisations reached out to the needy and excluded. In an increasingly pragmatic culture, the witness of Christian practice can be an effective way of understanding and expressing the presence of God. To do justice, the prophet Jeremiah says, is to know God. Engagement with the task of promoting a truly just world is for Christians a response to the call of the Reign or Kingdom of God. In the doing comes the understanding. Theologians need to learn by doing also and by being actively associated with the doers and seekers of justice, freedom, truth and peace. Studies such as these will, it is hoped, prove of help to religious thinkers who have not as yet had the opportunity for more active involvement in justice issues. Being drawn into that work their insights into the whole range of Christian doctrine and practice from the Trinity, Incarnation and the last things to environmental protection will be undoubtedly enriched. Out of that enrichment they will contribute in turn to the Christian perspectives on development work which Trócaire is in search of here.

At the same time there is the danger that such studies might become too self-enclosing or too bland or too negatively disputatious. With a good advisory team these particular dangers can be averted. So can the more subtle one whereby the work of a development agency of explicit Christian-Catholic inspiration is perceived as and/or becomes a vehicle for religious conversion. Trócaire, Cafod and SCIAF and similar agencies have, true to their mandate and to their genuine Christian inspiration, respected these distinctions very scrupulously. It would be very sad if its attempt to explore their theological roots were to obscure rather than clarify their integrity as a development agency devoted fully to the personal and social needs of the people they serve without any threat to the cultural or religious integrity of these people. It will therefore be a matter of real concern for the editor and authors of these studies to ensure that the renewal of Christian understanding and inspiration further protects and deepens the integrity of Trócaire, Cafod and SCIAF, and their work. In that also they will be making a further contribution to maintaining the varied vocation and work of the whole Church in the modern world.

Executive Summary

The second edition of this book, which includes a postscript by the author, explores the history and theology of human rights in the Catholic tradition. Its starting point is a statement of confidence in the concept and politics of human rights. It argues that despite the many limitations of the concept of human rights it remains our best attempt thus far to express some commonality, in a world of competing claims. The language of human rights insists that every individual has certain rights, not because of the position the person holds in that society, or because that person is the citizen of a particular state, but solely on the basis that s\he is a human being. Although it is only in the last 200 years that the concept of human rights emerged, the claims at the centre of human rights thinking are foundational to western society.

This paper examines the history of human rights thinking. It begins with an examination of the antecedents of human rights in Graeco-Roman and Jewish thought. It moves on to discuss the many ways in which the Hebrew Bible and New Testament carry in their teaching an inherent concept of human rights. It explores this idea further through Christian history, especially in relation to the Church's social teaching. It also discusses the political and philosophical developments of the seventeenth and eighteenth centuries which led to the explicit articulation of a concept of human rights. Although the Church was initially reluctant to endorse the concept of human rights, it eventually became one of its most important proponents. This text examines this recent history, from Leo XIII's encyclical *Rerum Novarum* to the many social encyclicals of the present pontiff.

The main components of the Catholic human rights tradition revolve around the centrality of the person, human rights as a way to safeguard human dignity in the social context, the correlation of rights and duties, the harmonisation of rights under the common good and the principle of subsidiarity. These continue to be developed and refined. The text ends with a discussion of the challenges which human rights pose for contemporary Christians. Human rights thinking challenges the Church to continue to be a prophetic voice on the world stage and to be an exemplar as well as an advocate of human rights. We are also challenged by those who critique the concept, to restore and develop the link, already present in Catholic thinking, between social justice and human rights. Moreover, we are challenged to develop a more historically and culturally sensitive concept of human rights. If we do so the concept and politics of human rights can become a universally recognised way of affirming the inherent worth and dignity of each and every human being.

lobalisation and human rights

The politics of human rights has grown in importance over the past five decades. The language has become widely accepted as the way in which we describe those things which all human beings hold in common. However this is not something which is easily done in contemporary society. Everywhere interest groups are drawing attention to their own particular concerns and there is an increasing reluctance to focus on shared or universal experiences. Indeed the dominant philosophical as well as political movements impel us to concern ourselves, not with questions of a universal nature, but with plurality and difference. This has been called "the time of the tribes", wherein we are oriented, not outwards to the global community, but to the local, the regional, the tribal. As a result the language of human rights has recently been viewed with suspicion. It is seen to represent yet another attempt by the west to impose its own philosophical system on the rest of the world. It is true that the language of human rights has emerged from the western philosophical and theological traditions. It is also true that it has occasionally been misused in global politics. However despite the many limitations of the concept of human rights it remains our best attempt thus far to express some commonality in a world of competing claims.

It is in this context that 1998 takes on great significance, for it is the 50th anniversary of one of the most important attempts in history to articulate that commonality. I am referring to the United Nations Declaration of Human Rights which represents a milestone in human history. 1998 is also the 25th anniversary of Trócaire which, in many respects is no less of a milestone for the Catholic Church in Ireland. In 1998 we recognise the founding of Trócaire as one of the many ways in which the Church in Ireland explicitly embraced work for justice, development and human rights as an integral part of its Christian mission. But 1998 is more than a commemoration of the founding of a particular agency. It also affords us the opportunity to reflect on the challenges which we face, now that we are on the threshold of the third millennium. The challenges for human rights are both practical and theoretical. On the practical level we are confronted with widespread violations of human rights for economic and political gain. On the theoretical level the concept of human rights itself has come under increasing attack, often for good reason. If the concept and the politics of human rights are to have a future then the first step is for people worldwide to rededicate themselves to both the idea and the reality of human rights.

The language of human rights is so common today that it is easy to assume that it has a long and illustrious history. Indeed one might assume that it forms a central plank of our self-understanding. However a historical analysis reveals that, although the idea of human rights may have been around in different guises for many centuries, the explicit articulation of human rights is a relatively recent phenomenon. Similarly it is easy to assume that Christianity's current endorsement of human rights is based on a longstanding affinity between the two. Again history suggests that this is not the case. In fact the Catholic Church was one of the most vocal critics of the concept of human rights for many years. At other times, of course, it has been an advocate and defender of human rights. Yet, although the terminology of human rights is no more than 200 years old, one of the legacies of the major world religions and philosophical traditions is a belief that human beings have a dignity and worth. This can be seen in different ways in Judaism, Christianity, Islam, Hinduism, Buddhism, Confucianism and Taoism. However it is also true that each tradition compromised and modified this belief in countless minor and sometimes significant ways. Almost all cultures and religions speak of the worth of human beings, yet they do so in ways which are particular to their context, and often with very different understandings of the person. Judaism and

Christianity speak of humans as being in the image and likeness of God, Islam speaks of the essential equality and freedom of all human beings and Hinduism envisages a life where each person brings about goodness and justice in the quest for self-enlightenment. Strictly speaking one could not claim that Islam, or Hinduism, or early Christianity have a theory of human rights. In fact the devotees of each religion may not recognise the terminology of human rights as part of their religious language. Yet they and the other religious traditions enshrine, in their beliefs and practices, the central claim of human rights, which is, that all human beings possess an essential dignity which is part of our makeup and which does not depend on external factors for its validity.

One could see the story of human rights as essentially one of the emergence of a shared language. The language does and can provide a way of expressing our best ideas about the nature of human beings and our relationships, ideas which are articulated in many culturally specific ways worldwide. It is a language which can be shared, which can express some of those things which human beings hold in common, without being too closely associated with any one religious tradition. Perhaps the greatest challenge for the politics of human rights as we prepare for the next millennium is that we recognise what we hold in common, that we respect those things which make us different and that we find strategies for relating across those differences. It is possible that human rights can be the vehicle for such a task. However it will only succeed if it is a language which emerges out of dialogue, and if it articulates a genuinely shared world-view. It cannot operate as an arm of western cultural, economic or political imperialism.

The history of human rights

Although it is only in the last 200 years that the concept of human rights emerged, the claims at the centre of human rights thinking are foundational to western society. The language of human rights insists that every individual has certain rights, not because of the position the person holds in that society, or because that person is the citizen of a particular state, but solely on the basis that s\he is a human being. It took many centuries for this claim to be explicitly articulated and still more for it to become widely accepted as legitimate. However, one can see very many milestones in the history of western thought which prepared the way for the radical declaration of the General Assembly of the United Nations on 10 December 1948, that "All human beings are born free and equal in dignity and rights" and that "Everyone is entitled to all the rights and freedoms set forth in the Declaration, without distinction of any kind, such as race, colour, sex, language, religion, political or other opinion, national or social origin, property, birth or other status".[1]

---

1 United Nations Declaration of Human Rights, Articles 1 and 2.

Antecedents of human rights thinking

The Graeco-Roman tradition

The Graeco-Roman philosophical tradition of the pre-Christian era established some important starting-points for human rights thinking. Although Greek society was a hierarchical one in which citizens enjoyed rights which non-citizens (including foreigners, women, slaves and children) did not, nonetheless it was out of this society that the idea and practice of democracy emerged. There are many ethical ideals which the philosophers of Greece bequeathed to western civilisation, but for the concept of human rights none is more important than the notion of natural law. This idea, formulated initially by the Stoics, suggests that there is a higher or ultimate law and justice to which all human law and behaviour is subject. Furthermore the Stoics proposed that we are able to discern this ultimate law through our reason. The Stoics believed that a person's moral responsibilities are not bounded by the state or city in which one lives. Expressing sentiments which seem remarkably modern the philosopher Zeno, who lived from 335 to 263 BCE, suggested that our lives should not be based on cities or peoples each with their own views of right and wrong, but that we should regard all people as our fellow citizens.

This concept was refined and developed by the Roman political orator Cicero (106-43 BCE). In his *De Republica*, a text which was to become the cornerstone of international law, he insisted: "And there will not be one law at Rome and another at Athens, one law now and a different one in the future, but there will be one law, eternal and unchangable which will bind all peoples at all times".[2] Although far from an elaborate doctrine of human rights, natural law established the basis for thinking about those elements which human beings

2 Cicero, *De Republica*

share. Furthermore it introduced a reference point outside of the particular society or community, to which indigenous law must be subject. It also proposed that this eternal, universal law or justice ought to be reflected in the particular laws and practices of each community.

The Hebrew Bible

The modern terminology of human rights is not found anywhere in the Hebrew Bible, nor in the rabbinic literature of Judaism. Nonetheless the Jewish tradition established some core ideas about the nature of human beings which form the basis of much subsequent thinking on human rights. All talk about human rights presupposes a recognition of the inherent worth of each and every human being. The Jewish tradition expressed the idea of the worth of humans by speaking of them as being *imago Dei* that is, created in the image and likeness of God. Like the rest of creation, human beings are valuable. Human beings are part of the created order, are not radically distinct or separate from it. As a result the interests of humans cannot be achieved at the expense of the rest of God's creatures. In the Hebrew Bible all of creation, including human beings, has an intrinsic worth.

However, in addition to possessing an inherent worth as part of God's creation, human beings are created in God's image. This extraordinary assertion by the biblical authors established a connection between human beings and their creator, with the source of absolute value. "Then God said, 'Let us make man in our image, after our likeness; and let him have dominion over the fish of the sea, over the birds of the air, and over the cattle, and over all the earth, and over every creeping thing that creeps upon the earth.' So God created man in his own image, in the image of God he created him; male and female he created them" (Gen.1:26-7). The impact of the text is remarkable. It enables each individual to recognise her\his own dignity and challenges us to see and respond to the image of God in each person we encounter. It establishes a fundamental equality among human beings, for regardless of one's social station, whether the person is the lowliest servant or the most regal of kings, each individual is first and foremost a creature in God's own image.

Although humans are essentially part of the created order, they have a unique place in it. They are to be stewards, caretakers of creation. However there is a tension in these texts. The focus on the uniqueness of human beings often means that their interests are given pre-eminence. Judaism and Christianity each struggle with the ethical implications of this model, especially in relation to the interests of the non-human world. Humans have real independence, free will and intelligence. This core freedom is a crucial component of the dignity of human beings. It allows us to shape our environment and to participate in the creation of our future.

This belief, which flowed from the conviction that humans are *imago Dei*, was given further force with the covenant between God and the people. The covenant was the most important religious event for the Jewish people. It brought them into an active partnership with God and established the special relationship between God and the community. The covenant is made after the exodus from Egypt. This of course is highly significant in thinking about human rights because the exodus itself can be interpreted as an instance of Yahweh's vindication of the rights of the oppressed. In many important respects the covenant reinforced the conviction that all human beings possess a special dignity. As *imago Dei*, humans are sufficiently God-like to enjoy a unique relationship with him. On the basis of their "godlikeness" they are called to an incomparable intimacy with God. This invitation to relationship confirms humanity's special place in creation. It expresses, in a profound way, our worth. Of course this covenant also calls for a response. Being in relationship with God calls for a life lived according to God's design. It places certain obligations on individuals and on the community. Fidelity to the covenant was expressed in many ways. The covenant's concern with social justice is a central component. In this one can see many antecedents of the human rights tradition.

"He has shown you, O man, what is good: and what does the Lord require of you but to do justice, and to love kindness, and to walk humbly with your God?" (Micah 6:8). The biblical concern for social justice was expressed in many ways. The community's religious and social structures were designed to embody God's mercy and justice. The law, which regulated the community's behaviour, institutionalised this concern with social justice. In Jewish law all persons should receive equal treatment: the rich are not favoured, they are legal equals with the poor. But Jewish law also recognised that one's social position could determine one's access to justice. As a result one finds an expression of special concern for widows and orphans, the poor and strangers. "You shall not wrong a stranger or oppress him, for you were strangers in the land of Egypt. You shall not afflict any widow or orphan." (Exodus 22 :21). The designation of these particular groups for special care arises from their vulnerability in the existing Jewish society and that of its neighbours. Widows and orphans, the poor and aliens (the refugees of the ancient world), each share an important characteristic: their powerlesness. They exert no power in society, they are dependent on the goodwill of the community and as such can easily be exploited.

Because of this, their interests were formally enshrined in the law. For example, a hungry traveller could go into any field and eat grain and grapes, as long as nothing, beyond what was needed, was taken. Similarly the poor, orphans, widows and travellers had the right to a portion of every crop. This included the edges of any field of grain, any fruit which had dropped to the ground, and all that the harvesters left behind after passing through the field once.[3] Other laws prohibited high interest rates for the poor and the payment of poor people for their work immediately on the same day. The understanding of justice is a dynamic and challenging one. Jewish law was oriented towards recognising a basic equality of all persons. More than that however, it recognised in its special provisions, that individuals and groups can also be marginalised by political and social practices. This realisation led to a number of concrete attempts to minimise this exploitation.

The prophets were the most outspoken advocates of justice for the poor and outcast. Justice is expected by God in response to his loving kindness. It is the way in which the community honours its fidelity to the covenant. It is impossible to enumerate the many dimensions of prophetic justice. The prophets built on existing obligations, but they infused them with an added urgency and dynamism. The prophets denounced all forms of privilege, confronted the religious and social elites with the demands of justice and urged Israel to return to the way of the Lord. They preached a message of radical justice and of the wrath of God if Israel did not transform its institutions. "Let justice roll down like waters, and righteousness like an ever-flowing stream" exhorts Amos (5:25). This justice is no mere mechanistic norm to be fulfilled but is an ever changing and evolving challenge. This demand to do justice is at the heart of biblical religion. It is not an optional extra but a requirement. It is the way in which the community responds to God's covenant. It is linked to a sense of human dignity which derives from the conviction that all human beings are *imago Dei*. Although not expressed in terms of rights, the Jewish tradition established a very profound sense of the

---

3 I have taken this information from an unpublished paper by David Smith entitled "New Testament perspectives on wealth and how it can be related to modern business", presented at the Association of Teachers of Moral Theology, Dublin, 1995

inalienable dignity of each individual, of the fundamental equality of persons, of the depth of human solidarity and of the special care due to the vulnerable and the marginalised. The vision of humanity elaborated in the Hebrew scriptures is an important precursor and foundation for the human rights tradition which emerged many centuries later.

The Jesus movement

Christianity developed out of Jewish culture and religion and Jesus' ministry was exercised in this context. The central message of the preaching of Jesus was the kingdom of God, which had social and economic, as well as religious implications. The gospels tell us that Jesus preached that the reign of God had already broken into human history. This kingdom required radical conversion and work for justice. The beatitudes recounted in Matthew develop a vision of the kingdom through those things which are expected of disciples of Jesus.

Blessed are the poor in spirit, for theirs is the kingdom of heaven.
Blessed are those who mourn, for they shall be comforted.
Blessed are the meek, for they shall inherit the earth.
Blessed are those who hunger and thirst for righteousness, for they shall be satisfied...
Blessed are you when men revile you and persecute you and utter all kinds of evil against you falsely on my account.
Rejoice and be glad for your reward is great in heaven, for so men persecuted the prophets who were before you.

(Mt 5:3-11)

These beatitudes express the fundamental dignity of all persons and reverse our traditional expectations. These surprising reversals leave Christians with a truly radical vision of the new order. The privileges and pomp of this world are meaningless, in fact are an obstacle to true insight. Work for social justice and the redistribution of riches is required of

Christians, and yet it is the poor and oppressed who are especially blessed. This demand that Jesus' followers put the interests of the outsider first is central to the gospel message. Action for justice, coupled with compassion and love are the ways by which Christians should be recognised. Jesus is described, especially by Luke, as the messianic liberator of the oppressed, as the one who fraternised with the outcasts, the prostitutes, prisoners and lepers. He is the champion of the poor and despised. This activity, which affirms the dignity of even the most abused, is also expected of Jesus' disciples.

The preaching of Jesus contained a double challenge. It insisted that Christians work for the coming of God's kingdom by implementing patterns of equality in social, economic and political relationships. This forms the basis of much Christian social teaching. However his message also requires us to look at the marginalised with new eyes, to see in them not failure and poverty, but God's blessing. By privileging the outcast, the gospel challenges us to see the inherent and inalienable dignity and worth of each person. The heart of the gospel message is that each person, no matter how despised and abused, is special in God's sight, possesses a value which can never be extinguished. Again, although not expressed in the language of rights, in this particular insight one can see an important precursor of human rights thinking. It challenges conventional ways of appraising an individual's worth. It disregards the usual hierarchies which value privilege and success. Instead Christians are taught to love one another, to do so not only in word, but also in deed, and to see in the poor and marginalised the face of God. For as Jesus taught: "As you did it to one of the least of these my brethren, you did it to me." (Mt 25:40)

Incarnation

The message of Jesus is but one aspect of his importance because Christians believe Jesus to be the Messiah, the Son of God, God Incarnate. This belief shapes the Christian moral vision. In the incarnation Jesus assumed humanity to himself, became human. In so doing he became an exemplar of how humans should live and be in the world. He is a model of perfect humanity and enables humans to see the true nature of our task in the world. Jesus is not just another prophet, reminding us of the obligations which we have to each other. He is God Incarnate who, in becoming human both teaches us how, and enables us to realise our full potential. Christians are thus required to imitate and participate in this God Incarnate in our lives. *Imitatio Christi* is our calling. He is revealed as a person "who is just, who is loving, especially towards the poor and oppressed, who seeks the freedom and liberation of all, and who is the source and substance of the unity and order in the universe".[4]

The doctrine of incarnation also has another significance. The fact that God assumed human nature in order to redeem it affirms the dignity of humanity in an extraordinary way. It reconfirms the Jewish understanding of human beings as *imago Dei* and gives it further force. Every person is the image of God, created by God and redeemed in Christ. We are called to recognise Christ in each person we encounter and to relate to them in a manner which respects their unique heritage. Furthermore we form a fundamental unity with one another, since we are, through his redemption brothers and sisters in Christ.

It is this understanding of the human person which allows one to speak of a Christian concept of human rights. Although it was not until the twentieth century that Christian denominations embraced the language of human rights, it had

---

4 D. Hollenbach, *Claims in Conflict Retrieving and Renewing the Catholic Human Rights Tradition*, New York, Paulist Press, 1979, p.116.

a latent theory of rights from the beginning. Religious doctrines and symbols, such as *imago Dei* and incarnation laid the foundations for a concept of personhood which is not only compatible with human rights thinking, but which develops it. Thus the nature of the person is the starting point of Christian thinking about human rights. The Christian recognises the essential dignity and self-sufficiency of each person. It is a dignity which does not depend on the acquisition of things or achievements for its validation.

The Christian believes that there are some fundamental and constant dimensions of the person which, in turn create certain obligations. Firstly one can speak of each individual as an embodied spirit. Human beings are corporeal, our bodies form a part of the integrated persons that we are. Christianity has always struggled with this. There has been a tendency to prioritise the spiritual aspects of human beings and to dismiss the value of the flesh. However the incarnation attests, in an excellent manner, to the value and importance of the body. The body is not merely an accessory. It is the ground of our subjectivity and the medium of all our experiences. All our knowledge is rooted in our corporeality. We know and value the world through our ability to touch, see and hear it. Our bodiliness mediates our connectedness with the world and with other embodied subjects.

This approach to the body is highly significant. It reminds Christians that the manner in which we treat our own bodies and those we encounter has ethical implications. If the body is the way we mediate our connectedness, then we must have reverence for the body. We must nourish and care for the body with as much attention as we would nourish the spirit. Furthermore we must attend to the basic needs of other embodied subjects by working towards the provision of the material conditions which all people require.[5] The basic needs

---

5 See the excellent discussion of basic needs in John Grindle's *Bread and Freedom: Basic Human Needs and Human Rights*, Trócaire and Gill & Macmillan, 1992.

of human beings, nutrition, shelter, work, and the freedom to create their future, must be fulfilled if the dignity of the embodied subject is to be concretised.

Respect and care for the body are not an optional extra but one of the ways in which the value of each person is affirmed. There are minimal conditions which must exist so the embodied person can live with dignity. If these conditions are denied to individuals, then we threaten their self-worth. It is not possible to talk in abstract terms about human dignity, as if it could exist theoretically. The inherent dignity of human beings, who are corporeal beings, must be concretised. If we are to respect human dignity, then part and parcel of this is respect for the bodily needs of the individual, since these form an integral part of what it means to be a person.

In addition to being an embodied spirit, the person is also inherently relational. Relationality is central to our humanity. We are not independent, isolated beings, but persons-in-relation. We are constituted by our relationships. Human beings are inherently social. Nothing living is totally self-contained. One cannot speak of an unrelated individual. Sociality is written into the core of our being. This primacy of relationship is also central to the Christian understanding of what it means to be human. It is confirmed symbolically in the creation narrative of Genesis when the author tells us that God said: "It is not good that the man should be alone" (Gen. 2: 18). As relational beings we are called to live in community. In order to do so well we must create a vision of how we can best structure this inherent sociality and enhance human dignity. Thus we struggle to establish institutions and patterns of behaviour which best serve human interests. This involves confronting those things which thwart human flourishing and which undermine relationships and destroy solidarity. This vision of the person in society leads to an ethic which respects the individual while recognising the centrality of relationship. Furthermore it implies the need for a social framework in which the needs and rights of individuals can be harmonised. Justice provides such a framework. The norms of justice combined with the activity of love establish the basis for the Christian's activity in the world. This activity must be directed towards the creation of an order which protects the dignity of human beings concretely.

Christianity also represents this relational pattern in its religious symbolism. Not only are human beings "persons-in-community", so too is God. The Christian God is a relational God, constituted in relationship and is a community of three persons. This symbolism sheds light on the way Christians view the world and the place of human beings in it. This trinitarian . theology articulates the belief that no one and no thing exists in and of itself, but does so in relationship with others. The vision of the created order is a communitarian one and is symbolically represented in Christianity's most important belief, that of the triune God. As *imago Dei,* human beings instance this relationality in every aspect of their lives. This symbol of God as three persons in a community of eternal love challenges human beings to embody this pattern in all our relationships. The force of this symbolism is to place mutual and loving relationships at the heart of the Christian calling.

The age of the Church fathers

The social consciousness which was evident in the biblical texts was continued in the early Church. There is no doubt that the Church fathers had a distinctive social ethic. This is especially true of the centuries before Christianity became the official religion of the empire. The age of the Church fathers usually refers to the first five centuries of Christianity. However within this time period one can identify many different phases. For our purposes one can distinguish two. The first relates to the early centuries when Christianity was one of a number of religious groups or sects within the Roman empire. The second saw Christianity become the religion of the state and an

integral part of public and political life. Obviously
Christianity's approach to social justice and what later became
known as human rights, changed as its relationship with the
state altered.

In the pre-Constantinian era Christianity's social concern
was mostly directed inwards. Christians were concerned with
developing an ethic for community living. There is
considerable scholarly debate about the nature of the early
Churches. Much of the debate centres around some passages
in the Acts of the Apostles which describe, either actually or in
an idealistic fashion, the first Christian communities. "Now the
company of those who believed were of one heart and one
soul, and no one said that any of the things he possessed was
his own, but they had everything in common." (Acts 4:32) The
community described here may indeed be a fictional one. But
whether communities like this actually existed or were aspired
to, is somewhat irrelevant. What is crucial is that in the early
centuries Christians shared a radical vision of how they ought
to live.

The writings of the Church fathers in the subsequent
centuries also attest to this fact. For example Justin, in his
Apology says: "We who loved above all else the way of
acquiring riches and possessions, now hand over to a
community fund what we possess and share it with every needy
person".[6] The redistribution of wealth through almsgiving,
especially to widows and orphans, was widely practised. So
too was care of the sick, of prisoners and of travellers. There
are also stories of the generosity and courage of Christians in
times of public disaster and plague,[7] of their hospitality to
strangers,[8] and many other acts of social justice and charity.
Although they did not oppose the system of slavery they did
show special consideration for the treatment of slaves.

6 Justin, *Apology*, 1. 14
7 Eusebius, *Ecclesastical Histories*, 7. 22. 9
8 Ibid., 4. 23. 10

Furthermore within the Christian communities all people were accorded equality of rights, regardless of whether they were slave or free. This was underpinned by the egalitarian formula of Galatians: "There is neither Jew nor Greek, there is neither slave nor free, there is neither male nor female; for you are all one in Christ Jesus" (Gal. 3:28). The vision of Christian life present in the texts of the early centuries had profound social and political implications. True the Christian communities themselves were often lacklustre in their attempts to implement it.[9] Nonetheless the vision of community, which clearly involved material as well as spiritual sharing, together with the treatment of slaves as equals (within the Church, if not in the broader social context), attests to a sense of social justice and human rights.

With the conversion of Constantine and the establishment of Christianity as the official religion of the empire the approach to social justice was altered. Although it is difficult to generalise, it is true to say that Christianity became absorbed by the state and at times itself became an instrument of oppression. This is very clearly seen in the treatment of non-Christians, or heretics as they were called.[10] On different occasions they were subjected to imprisonment, exile or torture. Yet the Church still considered itself obligated to alleviate the lot of the poor, sick and needy. It urged almsgiving, good treatment of slaves and charity to the sick, especially lepers. In their social teaching the Church fathers followed the gospels. They taught that social and economic relationships should be characterised by justice and charity, and that the common good of the society should take precedence over individual interest. They taught that human beings are equal, regardless of the social conditions of their birth, which are accidental. They also insisted that individuals who happen to be born into privilege were obliged to place their good fortune at the

---

9   See Paul's Letter to the Corinthians
10 It is worth noting here that this was not the first time heretics were persecuted.

service of those born into poverty and oppression.

The Church fathers, as we have already seen, did not condemn the practice of slavery as an attack on the essential dignity of persons. This lack of moral leadership on the part of the Church on this matter highlights the ambiguity of the history of the Church's involvement in human rights and justice. As a human institution, the Church has been limited by the socio-cultural ethos and the economic climate in which it has existed. It has at times condoned and endorsed social and economic inequalities. In addition it has often reinforced and replicated these unjust patterns in its own teaching and in its institutions. The acceptance of slavery is a vivid example of this. Instead of condemning it as a violation of the essential equality of human beings, the Church exhorted slaves to obey their masters "for the glory of God". In fact many theologians supported the Church's right to own slaves.

The Church's treatment of women is another case in point. Instead of denouncing misogyny, the Church itself was to the fore in perpetuating it. Views such as those of Augustine were commonplace. He claimed that "the woman, together with her own husband, is the image of God, so that the whole substance may be one image, but when she is referred to separately in her quality as a helpmeet, which regards the woman alone, then she is not the image of God, but, as regards the man alone, he is the image of God as fully and completely as when the woman too is joined with him in one"[11] thus contradicting the teaching of the scriptures.[12]

Thus the Church itself can claim no high moral ground. To be sure it was instrumental in establishing some fundamental beliefs about the dignity of human beings and their equality. In both theory and practice the Church was often associated with

---

11 Augustine, *De Continentia*, 1.23
12 The history of the Church's engagement with social questions over the centuries is extremely complex. I am acutely aware of the dangers of highlighting particular texts since it can obscure the variety of positions evident in the Church's tradition.

the poor and marginalised. However it did have some blind spots and occasionally functioned as an obstacle to equality. The heritage of the Hebrew scriptures and the gospels established some important antecedents for human rights thinking. Much of the subsequent doctrine of human rights is present, albeit in embryonic form, in Jewish and Christian thinking. However the Church struggled with its own limitations and there was often a gap between the egalitarian vision and its practice. The language and concept of human rights did not emerge from Christianity directly. The initial impetus was secular. Indeed, as we shall see in the next section, the Church reacted against the secular origin of human rights and was initially quite hostile to the concept.

Yet many of the ideas which were central to human rights thinking made their way into the political arena directly from Christianity. Although the philosophers and politicians who expounded these ideas were often unaware of their Christian heritage, or even contemptuous of it, the fact remains that the contemporary concept of human rights owes a great deal to the Judaeo-Christian idea that human beings share a fundamental equality and an inalienable dignity, by virtue of their being *imago Dei*.

Political and philosophical developments

There were of course many philosophical developments in the first millennium which are also antecedents to the human rights tradition. However these cannot be the focus of our enquiry, which is concerned with identifying the theological heritage of human rights. It is necessary at this point to mention a number of the political and philosophical developments which led directly to the emergence of the language of human rights.

An event which took place in England in 1215 CE is particularly relevant. In a text known as Magna Carta, King John agreed to grant his barons a number of rights. Although many of these were in fact specific political demands and not strictly relevant, and although these rights were to belong only to the barons, nonetheless it was significant. Its importance for future generations lay primarily in the granting of individuals the right not to be punished without due process of the law. The Habeas Corpus Act which was passed in 1679 gave legal force to the right granted in Magna Carta. This guarantee that imprisonment cannot take place without a legal hearing was also an important forerunner to the establishment of certain rights.

The seventeenth century in Europe and in the New World was a time of great philosophical and political inquiry. Various mechanisms to deal with the growing religious pluralism both in Europe and the United States contributed to the growing sense that individual liberty was an important value. The effects of the Protestant Reformation should not be understated in this regard. There was certainly no human rights agenda in the Reformation, but its political ramifications were highly significant.[13] For the first time Christian rulers had to confront the reality of a pluralism of religions in their jurisdictions. Of course there were Jews and Muslims living in Europe already. However the history of their treatment is less than edifying. They were rarely, if ever, given the right to follow their own religious traditions, although occasionally special arrangements were made for them.

With the Reformation however there was increasing pressure on rulers to allow some modicum of religious freedom. It developed slowly in some parts of Europe, but in the United States the reality of religious pluralism gave impetus to the gradual articulation of human rights, of which the right to religious liberty was a central component. The 1632 Charter of Maryland established the right to religious freedom, and other states followed suit, including Pennsylvania, which included the right to religious liberty in its "Frame of

---

13 I am grateful to Professor Haddon Willmer for pointing out that the significance of Protestantism is not limited to its political ramifications. It was also an occasion when the theological rootage of human rights thinking was being explored.

Government". The political fallout of the Reformation in England led eventually to another significant step in the evolution of human rights. William of Orange became king in 1688, in what was known as the Glorious Revolution. It was revolutionary in many respects, not least in that it depended on William's agreement to grant certain rights to his subjects. These rights, including that of religious freedom for Protestants, were granted in the 1689 Bill of Rights.

Alongside these political upheavals, philosophical thinking was developing apace. In the same year as the Bill if Rights, 1689, the great English philosopher John Locke published his *Two Treatises of Civil Government*. These texts were intended to articulate a philosophical justification for the Glorious Revolution of 1688. In addition to doing this, however, Locke also developed political theory in some important respects. Locke elaborated on the ancient concept of natural law and placed it at the centre of his political philosophy. In effect he argued that certain rights exist by nature. Indeed he spoke of all individuals as having rights to life, liberty and property. Furthermore he argued that respect for individual liberty should be endorsed in a general sense. The government should not merely tolerate the exercise of certain freedoms, rather it should allow individuals to exercise their right to liberty. This was an important step, both politically and philosophically. Up until this stage the exercise of rights was seen to depend on either the benevolence of the ruler or the kind of pressure which powerful groups could exert. Locke's *Two Treatises of Civil Government* resituated this entire process by arguing that particular rights, in this case life, liberty and property, belong to individuals by nature, and do not depend for their existence on their recognition by government. Locke's innovation was important in itself, but was given further impetus with political developments in France and America in the following century. There is no doubt that the revolutions in France and America consolidated and gave political expression to these embryonic ideas of human rights.

Towards the end of the eighteenth century a number of declarations associated with the American War of Independence began to articulate the concept of human rights. In 1774 the American colonies issued the Declaration and Resolves which enshrined Locke's claim that individuals have, by nature, a right to life, liberty and property. In 1776 the colony of Virginia also issued a Bill of Rights which claimed that all men are by nature equally free and independent and have certain inherent rights. This was essentially an early draft of the American Declaration of Independence of 1776 which claimed that all men are created equal, with certain inalienable rights including life, liberty and the pursuit of happiness. The subsequent War of Independence meant that it was not until 1787 that the American Constitution was adopted, and in 1789 amended with the American Bill of Rights, a very early catalogue of human rights.

The revolution in France, which began in 1789, had a similarly important role in developing thinking on human rights. In fact the revolution began with the Declaration of the Rights of Man and of the Citizen. This Declaration was intended to be universal in its scope. In its preamble it states that the representatives of the French people "have resolved to lay down... the natural, inviolable, legitimate and sacred rights of man", because corrupt governments worldwide refused to grant or recognise them. Furthermore it states that these rights are being declared "in the presence, and under the auspices of the Supreme Being". Then in the body of the text it details the rights which it believes belong to all men. These include liberty, safety and resistance to oppression, due process of law, religious freedom, freedom of thought and expression, democratic government and property. This declaration, coupled with the American Bill of Rights, marked a significant achievement in developing an understanding of human rights.

There is no doubt that the gradual decay of feudal society together with the revolutionary movements in France, England and America, gave impetus to the idea of the rights of man. In each case there was growing resistance to the idea of an absolute monarch who granted privileges and favours to his subjects as he saw fit. There were demands for some form of participation in government and some limits to the powers of rulers. The philosophers of the Enlightenment provided the theoretical basis for these political objectives. Jean Jacques Rousseau, Locke and others began to develop philosophies in which an individual's worth and dignity were not determined by whether that person was of noble birth or whether s\he was a serf. Furthermore, Enlightenment philosophers located the worth of all persons in the fact that human beings share a common humanity and that we are each rational beings. Thus the traditional distinctions based on one's heritage and social status were deemed to have no place in the new order. The explicit statement of the Rights of Man gave political expression to these ideas. These declarations of the Rights of Man asserted what was claimed to be a self-evident truth, that is, a truth that cannot be denied, that all human beings share a fundamental equality and that every form of government must be respectful of this. The hierarchical structure of the *ancien regime*, the old order, would not suffice in a world where all men share inviolable and sacred rights.

Of course such an idealistic expression of human intent had little success of implementation. There were political difficulties which the subsequent decades of revolution all over Europe attest to. But perhaps more fundamentally still were the limitations inherent in the declarations themselves. The Rights of Man was initially envisaged as just that, rights belonging primarily to men. Women were not deemed to possess these rights in and of themselves. The category of men was even more restrictive however, for, despite what the declaration claimed, all men were not in possession of such rights. In fact men who were not property owners, men who were slaves and children, joined the ranks of women who were excluded from these inviolable and sacred rights. Mary Wolstoncraft's *A Vindication of the Rights of Women* published in 1798 was a passionate argument against the self-imposed restrictions of the French Declaration. She argued that in the same way as all men were born equally free, so too should women be regarded to be in possession of these fundamental rights. The nineteenth and early twentieth centuries saw many political movements on behalf of those initially excluded from the Rights of Man. The rights were eventually granted, first to non-property owning males, then to slaves and lastly to women. These movements had varied success in different countries. It is very interesting to note that although a beacon of light in the late eighteenth century, France was one of the last countries in Europe to recognise that women too possess all the rights which men are due. In fact it was not until 1945 that women in France gained the right to vote in democratic elections. Still today there are concerns that the explicit rights of children are not adequately protected. As a result there have been many debates on children's rights as citizens. Likewise the issue of minority rights is coming to the fore, not only in Ireland, but also worldwide. In this there is a recognition that minority groups such as asylum seekers, immigrants and travellers may need special protection within the politics of human rights.

The experience of two world wars within thirty years gave political leaders a tremendous will to find some international mechanism for harmonising the aspirations of different countries. The establishment, in 1919, of the League of Nations was the first attempt to do so. It failed. However in the years immediately following on the second world war, there was a renewed effort to foster international co-operation and security. The Charter of the United Nations, framed in 1945, articulated such aspirations. As if to insist that international co-operation could not be achieved without recognising some fundamental human rights, the United Nations stated that part of its purpose would be to promote and encourage respect for human rights and for fundamental freedoms for all, without distinctions of race, sex, language or religion. The phrase "fundamental freedoms" was a reference to F. D. Roosevelt's celebrated address to Congress in 1941. In it he insisted that freedom of speech and expression, freedom of religion, freedom from want and freedom from fear should be recognised universally and should be secured everywhere. When the United Nations Assembly met in 1946 it set about introducing an equivalent Bill of Rights. The charter of the United Nations had affirmed that this was essential for the work of international co-operation. It instituted the United Nations Commission of Human Rights, presided over by Eleanor Roosevelt, and drew up the United Nations Declaration of Human Rights, which was adopted in 1948.

Of particular interest to Catholics is the fact that the future Pope John XXIII, then Monsignor Angelo Roncalli, who was Papal Nuncio in Paris, played a prominent role in drafting the Declaration. His commitment to human rights, exhibited at such an early stage, was to be one of the enduring legacies of his papacy. Indeed one could say that he was the pope who banished all previous Catholic anxieties about human rights, and articulated a Christian vision of human rights in his celebrated encyclical of 1963, *Pacem in Terris*. However the history of the Church's encounter with the philosophy of human rights will be examined in more detail in the next section.

The hopes implicit in the Declaration of 1948 began to fade rather quickly, when it became clear that the Declaration in itself was not sufficient to guarantee respect for human rights worldwide. The expectation that universal agreement on the basic inalienable rights of humans would facilitate world peace was somewhat idealistic. It ignored the difficulties of implementing these rights in practice, particularly in the context of political power and conflict. It is significant that at the time of the Declaration many states were still colonies. This needs to be borne in mind when looking at the contributions of particular states to the debates on human rights. The 1950's and 60's were years of struggle within the United Nations. The central difficulty with the Declaration of Human Rights lay in translating this rather aspirational document into a form which would oblige member states to implement it. In 1966 a number of texts were adopted, which together make up the International Bill of Rights, and which member states are expected to endorse. These are the International Covenant on

Economic, Social and Cultural Rights, the International Covenant on Civil and Political Rights and the Optional Protocol to the International Covenant on Civil and Political Rights. Over the decades a number of other important covenants have been adopted on specific aspects of human rights, yet these two covenants of 1966 remain a central plank of the universal recognition of human rights.

This short excursus through the history of the development of human rights has in some respects given a false sense of harmony at an international level. Although there was general agreement among many, but not all, of the signatories of the Declaration, there were also many points of disagreement. This is still the case especially between the countries which have liberal or democratic forms of government and those which have socialist or Marxist structures of government. The conventional perception is that the democratic states tend to emphasise the importance of civil and political rights, while the socialist states are primarily concerned with economic, social and cultural rights. Western nations focus on individual rights while socialist governments tend to stress the importance of collective rights. Rather than prioritising one philosophy of human rights and thereby risk alienating some governments, the United Nations distinguished the two sets of rights in the covenants. As a result nations could ratify one or both of the covenants. In short the United Nations gave states considerably more flexibility in terms of the nature and substance of human rights than was anticipated.

Development of a Catholic theory of human rights[14]

Modern Catholic thinking on human rights began with Pope Leo XIII, in particular with his groundbreaking encyclical *Rerum Novarum* of 1891. In this text Leo affirmed some of the basic tenets of the Church's subsequent teaching on social justice, and as a result, of human rights. The encyclical dealt with the condition of the working classes in industrial society. While it denounced all Marxist analysis, it did argue for the granting of certain rights to all workers. These rights were built on the recognition, explicitly developed in the encyclical, that all human beings have a natural right to procure what is required in order for them to live.[15] From this he went on to argue for a just or living wage for workers and for certain limitations on the rights of employers. But in addition to the case it made for these particular rights, *Rerum Novarum* also formulated a principle which was to have a more far reaching significance. This was the principle of the priority of the personal. In the words of the encyclical: "Man precedes the State, and possesses, prior to the formation of any State, the right of providing for the sustenance of his body".[16] This stress on the primacy of the interests of the individual over and above those of any state eventually became an important dimension of the doctrine of human rights. It suggested that, regardless of the ideological basis of the political or legal order, the state exists to serve persons, and not vice versa. It established the grounds for insisting that human beings can never be treated in an instrumental or utilitarian fashion, nor can their value be subordinated to any other end. The precedence of the person

---

14 This commentary on the development of Catholic social teaching is necessarily selective. I have focused only on the points in the encyclicals which are directly relevant. As a result many of the nuances and detail of the various texts have had to be ignored.
15 *Rerum Novarum*, 34
16 Ibid., 6

over the state is based on the claim that every single individual has to be respected for his or her inherent and inalienable worth.

However, commentators point out that certain tensions existed within this bold pronouncement. A difficulty existed with the absolute distinction Pope Leo made between the interests of the individual and those of the state. He failed to develop any sense that the state is constituted by individuals who are social beings, and that it functions to harmonise their interests in the light of the common good. This was something which later social encyclicals remedied. There were also tensions relating to the political consequences of this idea. In the encyclical Leo insisted that all persons share an essential equality. However he was nervous about the libertarian consequences of these claims, which were associated, in his mind, with the secularism and anti-clericalism of the French revolution. As a result he sought to minimise the democratic implications of his own thinking by endorsing the existing hierarchies in the social order.[17] Although this tension was not resolved properly until the middle of the twentieth century, Leo XIII's norm of the primacy of the person was a genuine source of insight in the development of an explicitly Catholic understanding of human rights.

The pontificates of Pius XI and XII (1922-58) also saw significant changes in Catholic social teaching and human rights. There were some theological innovations, but the main development of this period was the Church's gradual acceptance of the principles of democracy. In *Divini Redemptoris* Pius XI provided a list of the rights which every person is due. These were "the right to life, to bodily integrity, to the necessary means of existence, the right to tend towards one's ultimate goal... the right of association and the right to possess and use property".[18] He also tried to deal with the

---

17 Hollenbach, op. cit., p.46
18 Ibid., p.56

tension, already alluded to in *Rerum Novarum*, between the teaching on the basic equality of all persons and the Church's tendency to support the existing social hierarchies. Although he did not confront the inconsistency head on, he indicated that he was aware of the issue when he spoke of the ways in which social conditions can frustrate and limit human dignity and human rights.

Pius XI also developed and gave renewed importance to the concept of the common good which, although present in Catholic thinking before this, was not particularly prominent. In *Quadragesimo Anno* especially, Pius XI promoted the idea that the human rights of individuals must be harmonised under the common good. He insisted that people must respect each other's rights, fulfill their duties to one another and contribute to the common welfare of the community. There should not be an inherent conflict between the interests of the individual and the common good because the nature of the common good requires that all individuals share in that good. This concept of the common good is not equivalent to a utilitarian calculation of the greatest good. It is an attempt to harmonise the conflicting claims and interests of individuals, while recognising that each member of the community has a stake in the collective welfare.

Pius XI gave expression to another key concept in Catholic social teaching which has implications for human rights. This is the principle of subsidiarity which states that government or state intervention is justified only if it helps the individuals or smaller communities of which society is composed. This limits the power of the state to intervene in the lives of individuals and communities and gives them the power of self-direction. Thus "the limits of government intervention must be determined by the nature of the occasion which calls for the law's interference - the principle being that the law must not undertake more, nor proceed further, than is required for the remedy of the evil or the removal of the mischief".[19]   This essentially means that the persons most directly affected by a policy or decision or law should be centrally involved in its formulation.

Pius XII dealt with issues of social justice and human rights with tremendous vigour and enthusiasm. Indeed he addressed such questions more frequently than did any of his predecessors. As a result social justice became one of the central pre-occupations of the Church. He intervened in many political debates and engaged the Church more centrally in this sphere than any other pope before him. Although it is not possible to enter into debates about the adequacy of the Church's condemnation of Nazism and the protection of the Jews, one must keep in mind that this was a particularly dark period in history. The basis of Pius XII's vision for society was respect for human dignity, which he believed was a realisable moral imperative. His distinctive contribution was his belief that "although the moral claim that this dignity makes is unconditional, it is a claim which is structured and conditioned by the limitations and possibilities of persons in society. Furthermore the finite conditions which are necessary for the promotion of human dignity are human rights".[20] He analysed the operations of the major social institutions such as family, property and government specifically with reference to how they shaped human dignity.

On that basis he identified a number of human rights and corresponding duties. His Christmas address of 1942 is a typical example of his many statements on human rights. In that text he says that respect for human dignity entails respect for and the practical realisation of the following fundamental personal rights: the right to maintain and develop one's corporal, intellectual and moral life and especially the right to religious formation and education; the right to worship God in

---

19 *Rerum Novarum*, 35-36
20 Ibid., 59

private and public and to carry on religious works of charity; the right to marry and to achieve the aim of married life; the right to conjugal and domestic society; the right to work, as the indispensable means towards the maintenance of family life; the right to free choice of a state of life, and hence too, of the priesthood or religious life; the right to the use of material goods, in keeping with his duties and social limitations.[21]

The classic text for the Catholic doctrine of human rights is the 1963 encyclical of John XXIII, *Pacem in Terris*. It synthesised and developed many of the themes already elaborated in the preceding century. Whereas the approach of his predecessors was rather unsystematic and haphazard, that of John XXIII was highly formalised. That which set *Pacem in Terris* apart from all its forerunners was the fact that it laid out an explicit framework for a Catholic theory of human rights. The commitment to the concept of human rights is obvious from the opening paragraph. John XXIII began by insisting that: "Any human society if it is to be well ordered and productive, must lay down as a foundation this principle, namely that every human being is a person, that is, his nature is endowed with intelligence and free-will. Indeed precisely because he is a person he has rights and obligations flowing directly and simultaneously from his very nature. And as these rights are universal and inviolable so they cannot in any way be surrendered".[22] From here *Pacem in Terris* goes on to develop the consequences of this moral claim for society. It is extremely wide-ranging in its scope, discussing the impact of these claims on the relationships between individuals, between individuals and the state, between nations and the international community. The encyclical discusses the context of the correspondence between rights and duties. "A well ordered society requires that men recognise and observe their mutual rights and duties".[23] The individual's duties flow from the

---

21 Christmas Address, 1942, quoted in Hollenbach, op.cit., p.60
22 *Pacem in Terris*, 9

respect for human dignity which each person is due. Respect for human dignity is the basis of all the particular human rights to which individuals have a claim and which they have a duty to uphold.

Pacem in Terris then goes on to compose the most elaborate and systematic list of rights to which individuals may lay claim. Although the language is very reminiscent of the United Nations Declaration of Human Rights, the discussion of the basis of these rights is far more sophisticated and convincing. *Pacem in Terris* discusses these rights in different categories. They include rights relating to life and an adequate standard of living... the rights to life, bodily integrity, food, clothing, shelter, rest, medical care, necessary social services, security in case of sickness, unemployment, widowhood, or old age... Rights concerning moral and cultural values including rights to freedom of communication, to the pursuit of art, to be informed truthfully, to a basic education and higher education in keeping with the development of one's country. Rights in the area of religious activity... Rights in the area of family life... with equal rights for men and women, ...including rights to the economic, social cultural and moral conditions necessary to support family life... Economic rights including humane working conditions, a just wage, and the right to own property... Rights of assembly and association, to freedom of movement and to political rights including the rights to participate in public affairs and to juridical protection of all one's human rights.[24]

There have, of course, been important developments in the Catholic theory of human rights since 1963. However they each depend on the framework formulated in that encyclical. But one must see *Pacem in Terris* as an integral part of a tradition rather than as a radical innovation. The encyclicals of John XXIII's predecessors, together with the Church's traditional

23 Ibid., 31
24 Hollenbach, op.cit., p.66-7

commitment to social justice, contributed significantly to the Church's theory of human rights. Many of the foundational ideas about human rights existed in the earliest Jewish and Christian communities, albeit clothed in different terminology. The political and philosophical events of the eighteenth and nineteenth centuries also were influential in that they challenged the Church to accept the social and political implications of its own theological analysis. The Church could no longer teach about the inalienable dignity of human beings and the existence of human rights, while supporting hierarchical social institutions.

It is really with *Pacem in Terris* that one can see the Church making a radical break with its conservative past and being prepared to criticise existing social and legal institutions. Here it abandoned its traditional reluctance to criticise the status quo and was led by the demands of human rights and social justice. In this *Pacem in Terris* heralded a new era in the Church's approach to human rights. Although, as we have seen, the Church was indeed concerned with human rights issues from its very beginning, its commitment was somewhat limited by its natural inclination to protect the hierarchical ordering of society and to resist the radical social consequences of its own message. *Pacem in Terris* put human rights at the very centre of Christian social doctrine. It did this by insisting that, in the ever shifting social context the mechanism of protecting human dignity is human rights.

In the late twentieth century the Catholic Church has become a remarkable advocate of human rights. Vatican Council II was one event which extended the thinking of *Pacem in Terris*. In *Gaudium et Spes* the Church developed its thinking by explicitly affirming that the dignity of persons can only be affirmed in the concrete conditions of history. In so doing the Church acknowledged two important realities. First it suggested that using the language of human rights is not sufficient, recognising that its commitment cannot be purely theoretical, but must also be executed in practice. Secondly, in acknowledging the importance of the historical context, *Gaudium et Spes* places responsibility with individuals and communities, to read the signs of the times and to determine the precise form which human rights should take in the concrete circumstances of political and social life.[25] This recognition is significant because it suggests that the articulation of the content of human rights must be context-sensitive, and must take account of the social and political conditions of existence. Thus human rights cannot be identified exclusively with any particular political ideology or form of government. The specific manner in which human dignity is realised through human rights may differ in each context. This is the inevitable implication of recognising the important role of cultural and historical conditions in the development of human rights. *Gaudium et Spes* provides an important impetus for the development of a context-sensitive theory of human rights.

Another influential document of the time was *Populorum Progressio*. This was a social encyclical and not one of the documents of the Council. However it too is highly significant in terms of the growing sophistication of Catholic human rights thinking because here the Church explicitly addressed structural and institutional concerns. *Populorum Progressio* emphasised that poverty is a worldwide issue which needed to be tackled on a global scale. It introduced the concept of development to Catholic thinking and argued for radical change in order to combat the inherent institutional injustices in the world's economic and political order.

Vatican II will also be remembered for the dramatic shift in the Church's attitude to religious freedom. This issue has been closely allied with human rights from the very beginning. Among the rights which were enshrined in the American

---

25 Trócaire's commitment to reading the signs of the times was reiterated in its 25th Anniversary Declaration.

Constitution was the right to religious freedom. However, although the Church benefited from this freedom, it was still influenced by its own tradition of error having no rights. In this case error could mean any religious tradition or denomination other than Catholicism. *Dignitatis Humanae* reversed this completely and recognised the right to religious freedom as an important human right. In so doing it dissolved one of the most glaring inconsistencies of the Church's human rights tradition.

Vatican II had many other important implications for the tradition of human rights. Perhaps the most important was the impetus it gave to the emergence of liberation theology. Associated primarily with Latin America in the early years, liberation theology has subsequently grown to be a context-sensitive, justice-oriented coalition of theologies from every part of the globe. Liberation theologies articulate the demands of social justice and human rights from the perspective of the marginalised. It is the experience of the poor in history and not the logic of academic debate, which shapes and forms the myriad theologies which have emerged "from the underside of history". The specific contribution which liberation theology has made to the Catholic theory of human rights is that it has insisted that the interests of the marginalised should be at the heart of the Christian vision and that political work for justice is a requirement of the gospel. The preferential option for the poor and the denunciation of all forms of economic and social privilege are regarded as the ways in which the Christian should work for the establishment of the kingdom on earth. Liberation theologians, such as Gustavo Gutierrez, Ivonne Gebarra, Jose Miguel Bonino and many others, helped the Church to clarify the uncompromising nature of its work for human rights.

There are many other aspects of liberation theology which have had an impact on the way in which the Church has subsequently conceptualised and implemented its work for social justice. In fact for all his warning to the liberation theologians, one can see very clearly that in his social encyclicals, Pope John Paul II has been significantly influenced by their theology. It is difficult to convey the enormous impact which liberation theology has had on the Church's understanding of human rights. To a certain extent the main ingredients of its approach have been evident in the Christian tradition from its beginning. So too was the full blown theology of human rights already expressed in *Pacem in Terris*, which was published almost a decade before Gutierrez's seminal work of 1971, *A Theology of Liberation*. Nonetheless, when liberation theology exploded onto the theological stage, it relocated the entire discussion about human rights. The analysis transformed the traditional approaches and gave them new vigour. In addition it led to the reconceptualisation of the Christian understanding of mission, replaced the work of charity with justice and developed the kind of vision which was the basis of the new style of Catholic development agency. Working for the implementation of human rights worldwide, especially for those who are unable to articulate and claim those rights for themselves, is now regarded as an essential element of Christian discipleship. In some senses one might say that thinking on human rights has come a full circle in that the radical vision of the earliest Christian communities is that which contemporary Christians are inspired to pursue, except that now it is on a global scale.

In the pontificate of John Paul II, Catholic thinking on human rights and social justice has become sophisticated, subtle and passionate. He has produced an extraordinary number of encyclicals and addresses which have dealt explicitly with human rights issues worldwide. His commitment to human rights as the way in which human dignity is promoted is unequalled in Catholic history. In many respects this can be seen as a reflection of the status which the language of human rights has acquired on the world stage. It is now considered to be the way in which governments, organisations and individuals can work to promote human well-being. It is certainly the case that the Catholic Church has contributed to growing acceptance of the language of human rights as the way in which human beings can express our equality and solidarity. The other feature of the social encyclicals of John Paul II noteworthy from this perspective, is the degree of economic, social and political expertise which they exhibit. As a result they are serious and convincing documents, not mere rhetoric or utopian sentiment. John Paul II has reiterated, on every possible occasion that honouring and implementing human rights is the responsibility of individual citizens and of governments and that, furthermore, it is a responsibility which is demanded by the challenge of being human, that is created in God's own image.

The challenge of human rights

The centrality of the person, human rights as a way to safeguard human dignity in the social context, the correlation of rights and duties, the harmonisation of rights under the common good and the principle of subsidiarity are the main components of the Catholic human rights tradition. They each have their roots in the earliest texts and traditions of Christianity and were gradually developed, in the twentieth century, into a comprehensive doctrine of human rights. Today human rights are an integral way of understanding and expressing the demands of being Christian. The concept of human rights is not a particularly Christian one. As we have already seen the first and most explicit expressions of the idea that human beings possess certain inalienable rights were secular. Indeed the context was not only secular, but overtly hostile to Christianity. This was because, in the minds of many, Christianity was associated with the privilege and hierarchies of the old order, in which many people were denied any rights at all.

The Church initially reacted to the anti-religious tenor of the new democratic spirit and denounced the politics of human rights. Pius VI, in his *Quod Aliquantum* of 1791 pronounced that it was anathema for Catholics to accept the 1789 Declaration of the Rights of Man and of the Citizen. He actually believed that the Declaration was a conspiracy to end the predominance of the Catholic Church in France. He claimed that "this equality, this liberty, so highly exalted by the National Assembly, have then as their only result the overthrow of the Catholic religion".[26]

Nonetheless Christianity provided many of the key philosophical ideas which enabled the formulation of the

---

26 See the excellent article by Bernard Plongeron, "Anathema or dialogue? Christian reactions to declarations of the rights of man in the United States and Europe in the Eighteenth Century", in Alois Muller and Norbert Greinacher, eds., "The Church and the Rights of Man", *Concilium*, no., 12, New York, Seabury, 1979, pp.1-16.

concept of human rights. It would be inaccurate to suggest that Christianity alone provided the building blocks. However it is true that the Christian understanding of the person as free, equal, embodied and relational was one which infused western philosophical and political thought. It was this understanding of the person, above all else, which was the foundation of all subsequent developments of human rights.

The development of a Catholic doctrine of human rights is very significant, especially for the Church itself. It has enabled Catholics to understand that their own praxis, inspired though it may be by their Catholicism, is part of a larger commitment which all human beings can share. It is not a provincial or local language, rather it is one which unites them with people of many creeds and none. But in addition to bringing the Church into a dialogue which is shared universally, the theology of human rights also highlights some of the distinctive and unique aspects of the Christian message. Indeed many of the challenges which confront the Church vis-à-vis human rights relate to developing both these aspects. Human rights can teach us about those things which human beings hold in common. In addition it can focus our attention on the ways in which Christianity can make a distinctive contribution to the language and politics of human rights. In this final section I will discuss what I consider to be some of the most fundamental challenges which the theology of human rights brings.

Although there are many more issues which also warrant attention these are, in my opinion the most central. The theology of human rights challenges the Church to continue to be the protector of the vulnerable and a prophetic voice and imagination in society. Furthermore it confronts the Church with the reality that in order to be a credible witness to human rights it needs to be an exemplar. It must incarnate, both within its own community, and in its relations with others, its commitment to human rights. In this the "politics of forgiveness"[27] are paramount. A further concern, which actually has profound implications for the politics of human rights on the world stage, is the evolving nature of our understanding of human rights. As is obvious from the history of human rights, the concept adapts and changes in response to various social, political and historical conditions. The Catholic tradition can make a distinctive contribution to this especially in relation to the way in which the Catholic theory makes strong links between its doctrine of social justice and the nature of human rights. The final point which demands our attention is the challenge which the politics of human rights brings to our engagement with the variety and diversity of the cultures, religions and traditions of the world. In the age of globalisation some kind of global responsibility, based on shared values is vital. The politics of human rights may indeed be an important starting point for such a project, though it is not without its limitations.

---

27 I borrow this phrase from Haddon Willmer who developed this idea in "The politics of forgiveness - A new dynamic", *The Furrow,* 1979, pp.207-18.

1 A prophetic voice

It is obvious that now, at the end of the twentieth century, the Catholic Church has a strong and convincing doctrine of human rights. It also has a significant number of commissions and development agencies (such as Trócaire) working for the establishment of justice and the recognition of human rights worldwide. This pattern of theological reflection combined with active political engagement is one which the Church has only slowly developed. True, the Church has always been engaged in missionary activity and has been associated with charitable works. However one of the consequences of the Church's social teaching, especially since *Populorum Progressio*, has been the establishment of formal Church agencies to promote and participate in the work for justice. The significance of this lies with the Church's recognition that work for justice, and not simply charitable works, is how the Christian realises her\his calling in society. Furthermore there is the realisation that this work ought not simply to be done at an individual level, but should have a formal and institutional aspect. This means that work for human rights and social justice is written into the heart of what it means to be Church. It is not an optional extra, nor is it purely the responsibility of individual Christians. It is a core dimension of our struggle to be Church.

The theology of human rights then, challenges the Church to continue this commitment to human rights as integral to the work of the gospel. It is a task which demands not only courage and perseverance but also political acumen and wisdom. Being the voice for the voiceless requires a great degree of sensitivity. Those who are voiceless do not easily come to our attention. They can also be the victims of the short attention-span of the western media. The Kurdish refugees in Iraq are one such group whose human rights have been violated and who, despite a brief surge of concern some years ago, remain voiceless. The victims of violence in Rwanda, in East Timor, in Algeria and elsewhere are similarly voiceless and therefore dependent on others to argue their case for them. So too are the victims of famine in Sudan and elsewhere. In seeking to protect the most vulnerable and disadvantaged the Church also needs to be attentive to the potential blindness which may cloud its vision. This is often the case in relation to situations which are familiar and close to home. In the Irish context the plight of refugees, the discrimination and abuse which they suffer, both from state institutions and private citizens, challenges the Church's commitment to human rights. If the Church locally is really to be the voice of the voiceless, then the interests of refugees in Ireland ought surely to be of primary concern. Its interventions on behalf of refugees to date have indeed been challenging and prophetic. The same could be said of the human rights of the travelling community who similarly challenge the Church's commitment to especially protect the vulnerable and to respond to their needs.

This kind of action often means that the Church may alienate some people. Not only in the wider society, but also in its own community. However the prophetic voice of the Church should expect to make people uncomfortable because it challenges individuals and communities to revisit long held views and prejudices. This is something which is often said but rarely experienced. This is because the faithful tend to be selective about the preaching we hear, the Church tends to be hesitant about engaging in local politics and it is easier to be more willing to apply the demands of justice and human rights to people and places far from our own. We can argue passionately about the human rights abuses in Colombia, Nigeria, Burma or Chile, but ignore those on our doorstep. We disregard the implications of the theology in our own immediate context. Again these are inconsistencies which need to be highlighted, which the prophetic Church is challenged to denounce. Although the theology of human rights may be in place and easily accepted in the abstract, the challenge to implement and live the demands remains a constant struggle.

2 Human rights in the Church and its relationships

In order for the Church to be a convincing proponent of human rights it must not only preach about their importance it must also embody that commitment in its own practices and relationships. This is and has long been an area of contention within the Church itself. Since the articulation of its human rights agenda the Church has been besieged with demands, from its own members, to extend this commitment to its own patterns of behaviour. This is especially true of a number of areas including the role of women, which have been understood as human rights or justice issues within the Church.

Although the Church has endorsed the language of human rights as a means of preaching its message of justice to and in the world, it is still very unclear how this is to apply to the internal life of the Church. One of the frequent responses to this issue is that the Church is not a democracy and that the language of rights has no place in the Church. The underlying basis for such a reaction is a sense that the Church is unlike other social institutions and therefore should not be governed by the same principles. It argues that the adoption of the norms of secular organisations would assimilate the Church to the state and would fundamentally alter its character and its uniqueness. A rather extreme version of this response draws a sharp dualism between the Church and all other social institutions and suggests that the Church is a divine institution with its own ordering and structures. The principles and norms, including those of justice and human rights, which the Church regards as so important in the secular world, are deemed to have no place in the institutional Church.

Although there may be reasons why the language of rights may be inappropriate or incomplete in the context of the institutional Church, such a radically drawn distinction between the secular and ecclesial life of the individual is unhelpful. Such a dualism functions to denigrate the importance of the secular life of the individual and suggests an attitude which is contrary to the one expressed in *Gaudium et Spes* which speaks, again and again, about the revelation of God's purpose in the development of human society. To inaugurate a dualism between these two spheres does seem to go against the understanding of the essential unity of the person. John Langan highlights the contradictory nature of this position when he asks: "Are we to suppose that human development proceeds along radically different lines once we enter the ecclesial sphere - and that the innermost truth about humanity is at odds with the development of human personality and human rights?"[28]

In an effort to avoid this dualism, it is often suggested that the Church as a voluntary association can require its members to forego certain rights. The popular manifestation of this position is that the Church is like a club, one must abide by the rules or else not be a member. Although there may be an extent to which this "voluntaristic" understanding is viable, it is not without its problems. This view does not address the problem of the Church's occasional failure to implement its own agreed practices. For example *Gaudium et Spes* teaches that "in order that such persons may fulfill their proper function (viz. theological enquiry and teaching), let it be recognised that all the faithful, clerical and lay, possess a lawful freedom of enquiry and of thought, and the freedom to express their minds humbly and courageously about those matters in which they enjoy competence".[29] However recent experience suggests that the Church has a genuine difficulty in operating according to its own requirements. Nor is this exclusively a modern problem. The history of the Church's treatment of those whose ideas have challenged the prevailing scientific, literary or

---

28 J. Langan, "Human rights in Roman Catholicism" in Curran and McCormick, *Readings in Moral Theology No. 5, Official Catholic Social Teaching*, New York, Paulist Press, 1985, p.125
29 *Gaudium et Spes*, 62, quoted in Walf, "Gospel, Church law and human rights : Foundations and deficiencies", *Concilium*, 1990/2, p.38.

historical consensus is rather bleak. Such failures suggest that the institutional Church is all too prone to the failures of any human institution and thus ought to take measures to protect the human dignity of its own members. And since it has said, again and again, that the vindication of human rights is the way in which the person's dignity is protected in the social context, it is difficult to accept the Church's reluctance to endorse human rights in its own structures

The language of rights may be inappropriate for the Church. The notion of vindicating the moral claims of the individual may be too minimalist for a community which seeks to be a sign of God's kingdom on earth. The common response is that the relationships within the community ought to be characterised by love and not merely justice. This certainly may be the way in which the Church promotes human dignity, that is by attending, not to the minimal requirements of human rights, but by expanding and enriching them. However, loving and mutual relationships do also respect the minimal conditions for the promotion of human dignity. That is it is not possible to disregard or ignore the basic requirements in the name of promoting something more substantial. Thus, although the language of human rights may be too legalistic or abstract for the Church, it is not because these rights have no place in the Church, but because they do not require enough of us.

The theology of human rights also challenges the Church in its relationships with other denominations and religions. This is not to suggest that we should expect agreement between different religious traditions or Christian denominations on every important issue. There are substantial differences which cannot be glossed over, nor should we expect them to be. However it is the manner in which the Church conducts its relationships and engages with perspectives which it does not share, which is crucial in this respect. The Church preaches that although the protection of human dignity is a universal requirement it may take different forms in different cultural contexts. Furthermore it recognises that there is a plurality of ways of being religious and indeed of being Christian. In addition it has accepted that respectful dialogue between denominations and religious is essential in the modern world. And yet its own relations, particularly with denominations so similar to itself are too often not instances of respectful dialogue. As the Church becomes more comfortable with the language of human rights it is also challenged to embody this respect for human dignity in all its relationships. In order to be a convincing voice for its own theology of human rights the Church must be an exemplar of the position it preaches.

3 Human rights and social justice

It is widely acknowledged that, although most of the world's countries have signed up to the United Nations Declaration of Human Rights, there are many problems with the content. Specifically many scholars and activists have criticised the Declaration on the basis that it has an overly western bias, and that it does not always reflect the values and concerns of the non-western world. Of course this is somewhat inevitable since the Declaration emerged out of the political and philosophical traditions of the west. It not only implied a preference for certain forms of government and political ideologies, it also contained many specifically western understandings and values, of which it was unaware. The United Nations was challenged initially by the former communist countries to be more self-critical and more aware of its own interests and biases. The issue on which this debate was conducted was on the nature of human rights and the communist bloc's belief that there was an excessive focus on the individual's political rights, to the exclusion of economic, social and cultural rights.

The United Nations sought to rectify this by preparing two different, but equally important statements to which the countries could sign up. These, as we have already mentioned, are the International Covenant on Economic, Social and Cultural Rights and the International Covenant on Civil and Political Rights. Although this affirms that there can be different ways of protecting human dignity and human rights, many commentators believe that it has not done so sufficiently. Fifty years on many of the southern nations have joined the former communist and socialist states in their criticism of the failure of the Declaration to reflect sufficiently their values and world-view. The objection continues to be focused on the manner in which the Declaration, and indeed the whole concept of human rights, tends to prioritise the interests of the individual, to the exclusion of all other concerns.

Chandra Muzaffar, a former prisoner of conscience himself, has argued that human rights, as understood by most in the west, are synonymous with political and civil rights. The right to freedom of speech, to a free press, to democratic elections are frequently considered by westerners to be the measure of a country's commitment to human rights.[30] Instead he argues for an expansion in our understanding of human rights and to give equal priority to, for example, economic rights. The right to food, to health, to shelter, to clothing, can be of far greater importance to those who are without any of these, than the right to a free press. Of course, as Walden Bello makes clear, the dichotomy is in effect a false one. In his article "Democratic expansion and democratic deepening in South-East Asia"[31] Bello highlights the fact that economic, cultural and civil rights form a kind of seamless web. Countries which focus on economic growth, but which deny the majority of citizens civil freedoms, rarely share the economic gains with the people either. The essential unity of all these rights is something which western countries too need to recognise.

The Catholic theory of human rights expresses this linkage between social justice and human rights excellently. It has long recognised that individual civil freedoms, without an equitable and just social order are meaningless. Indeed throughout the history of the theology of human rights, from the early centuries of Christianity, and in the Hebrew Bible, one can see that the abiding commitment is to social justice. Civil and political rights are an important component of a just social order, but are not the only nor necessarily the first concern. The inherent link between the two is based on the conceptualisation of the person which lies behind the theology. The person is understood, not as an utterly independent and disconnected individual, but as a relational and social being. This

---

30 C. Muzaffar, "Rethinking the concept of human rights", *Idoc Internazionale,* 4/93, p.8
31 *Trócaire Development Review,* 1997, pp.25-38

understanding means that these aspects of human life are not marginalised, rather they are central to any discussion of how human dignity can be promoted. In the Christian tradition human rights can never be divorced from the wider questions of social justice. Nor can human rights be reduced to individual political rights. The exclusive focus on civil rights ignores the embodied nature of human beings. Such impulses fundamentally contradict the Church's basis for human rights, which lies in the rich and complex understanding of the human person which the Christian tradition promotes.

4 Human rights and a global ethic

Human rights language is based on the central belief that there
are some things which all human beings share, regardless of
their culture, religion, race or gender. However this belief has
come under significant attack over the past decade. The
attack has come mainly from the academy, in the guise of
postmodernism. Postmodernism has highlighted some grave
deficiencies in the manner in which academic and political
debate has traditionally been conducted. Specifically it is
sceptical about the possibility of any objectivity in knowledge
and urges us to abandon all pretensions to universality. It
promotes a vision of human beings as fragmented, plural and
radically different. The original impetus was indeed necessary.
It arose out of the recognition that many voices and
perspectives are marginalised, in the name of the universal.
Thus postmodern theory sought to celebrate the plurality of
human existence, not to obliterate it. However, ironically,
instead of liberating us from the narrowness of our own
perspectives, postmodernism has locked us into local
subsystems of belief. This is because it has promoted a view of
human beings as radically different from each other, one which
sees values as incommensurable and one which rejects the
possibility of any cross-cultural criticism or engagement. We
are told that human beings are so shaped and determined by
their own experiences and cultural boundaries that they can
never really transcend them.

   Clearly this vision of human society profoundly challenges
the idea and the politics of human rights. Of course
individuals and communities need to recognise that they are to
some extent the products of their environment. Of course no
particular culture or religion has a monopoly on the truth. Of
course one can never completely understand a culture or
tradition from the outside. But these realities should not deter
us from attempting to articulate our commonalities, from
engaging with traditions which are not our own, nor from

criticising a specific culture for failing its people in particular ways. Otherwise each individual would be the victim of its own cultural dominance, without any prospect of external reference.

The human rights tradition, from its very beginnings in the Stoic idea of natural law, has been based on the conviction that, regardless of the views of different cultures, individuals do have certain rights. Furthermore their claim to have these rights vindicated does not depend on the agreement of a particular government, religious authority or culture. These are rights which the individual possesses by nature and which social and political institutions are duty bound to honour. Yes, there are philosophical problems with this. There are also political difficulties, particularly associated with the west's imperialist past and the suspicion that the human rights agenda, as it is currently expressed, prioritises the values of the west over all others. However these are concerns which the human rights tradition can indeed address.

Our understanding of human rights certainly needs to be more historically and culturally sensitive. It needs to take account of the many ways in which power relations infuse academic as well as political discourse. Furthermore it needs to hear alternative and dissident opinions and to engage with them. Yet with all its ambiguities the concept of human rights represents the best chance we have of protesting injustice and of protecting human dignity. It contains within it the conviction that the things that human beings share are more fundamental than those things which divide them. It articulates "the dream of a common language"[32] and the hope that dialogue and mutual engagement will enable us to overcome division. Most importantly however it is a universally recognised way of affirming the inherent worth and dignity of each and every human being.

---

32 This is the title of a collection of poems by Adrienne Rich.

Christian Perspectives on Development Issues: Human Rights

Postscript

In the few years since this text was produced there have been many significant developments that have a bearing on the manner in which human rights are discussed. The profile of human rights language continues to rise, while at the same time human rights violations appear to grow in frequency and intensity. The events of September 11th and the subsequent war in Afghanistan cast a long shadow over the politics of international relations, raising concerns about compliance with the humanitarian laws of war and international human rights standards. While huge numbers of people continue to live in abject poverty, the majority of the world's rich or donor nations have failed to set out a timepath for reaching the 0.7% aid to GNP target set by the UN back in 1970. At the same time the world's most heavily indebted countries have only received limited debt relief. Despite some positive developments in the availability of retroviral drugs, the HIV/AIDS pandemic has wreaked havoc on the social, health and economic infrastructure of many developing countries, to say nothing of the human misery and suffering caused by the pandemic. War, poverty and disease all create situations in which human rights are threatened and, in the process, increase people's vulnerability. Thus, as they encapsulate the shared language of protest, human rights will continue to have a significant role to play in efforts to shape a better world.

In her capacity as United Nations Commissioner for Human Rights, Mary Robinson has spoken frequently about the indivisibility of human rights[1]. She has recognised as legitimate

---

1 See for example Mary Robinson. "Dialogue, participation, partnership", in Ceide, Vol. 5, No. 4, February/March, 2002, p. 8

the concern expressed by some countries (particularly in Africa and Asia) that civil and political rights have been given disproportionate attention, while economic, social and cultural rights are often ignored. Indeed it seems that, in the three decades since the two International Covenants came into force, the division between these two elements of human rights regimes has become even greater. This is certainly true at the level of the politics of human rights world-wide. For example it has been the position of a number of Asian leaders in the 1990s that their populations are prepared to sacrifice civil and political liberties in exchange for greater economic security. Moreover they have continued to hold this position despite the protestations of dissidents within their own countries. In the United States of America, by contrast, the constitutional protection of civil and political rights (even post September 11th 2001) has continued to obscure its poor record in securing economic and social rights, particularly for its minority populations.

There is no doubt that the particular historical and political reality of each country predisposes it to implement human rights norms in a particular way. Yet the concept of the indivisibility of rights means that every country is challenged to look first at its own record and to attend to the lacunae there. This means that, while Indonesia, for instance, would need to be attentive to its failures in civil rights, the US would also need to examine how its own minorities often lack basic rights to shelter and healthcare. While there is much still to be done to promote the indivisibility of rights, a historical view reveals that significant strides have been made both politically and philosophically over the past decade. Democratic governments can no longer simply point to the existence of a free press or the right to free association as clear evidence of their commitment to human rights. They now recognise that access to adequate shelter, healthcare and social services for the entire population is also relevant to the case. Philosophically the language of human rights has been virtually divested of its initial and almost exclusive focus on civil and political rights. The role of the United Nations has been pivotal here. It has advanced the idea that 'civil and political rights in isolation are largely meaningless without respect for economic, social and cultural rights[2]', and its recent declarations on the rights of the child and those of indigenous populations[3] have further developed this linkage in imaginative and compelling ways.

Although many significant developments have taken place, the gap between the rhetoric of human rights norms and the reality of their implementation seems wider than ever. An analysis of the reasons for this growing chasm (despite significant gains in certain areas) is well beyond the scope of this postscript. Nonetheless, one can highlight a few global trends that go some way towards explaining this. Some features of globalisation threaten the, often minimal, achievements arising from the politics of human rights. The acceleration of environmental degradation, the destruction of indigenous cultures, the commodification of natural resources and labour, the nomadic practices of multinational corporations which move in and out of countries at will in search of still higher profits, all of these compromise people's human rights. Once we recognise that poverty is the most endemic violation of human rights and the most serious obstacle to achieving human rights for all, then we see that the growing power of transnational corporations and international bodies (such as the World Trade Organisation (WTO) and the International Monetary Fund) is also of significance. These institutions thrive in the context of globalisation, given their influence on international economic policy formulation. Yet the perceived democratic deficit in each of these bodies, together with concerns that certain developed countries still wield disproportionate power, means that they are viewed by some as negative features of a global market.

2 Trócaire 25 Declaration, Trócaire Development Review, 1998, p. 8.
3 See www.unhchr.ch/html/intlinst.htm

The trend towards 'global governance' doubtless presents the human rights lobby with an opportunity to mobilise global civil society to pursue an ethical form of globalisation[4]. However, there are also a number of potential hazards to the achievement of human rights. First of all the norms and principles which govern the operations of these international financial organisations in practice often conflict with their stated poverty-reduction objectives and strategies. The impact of structural adjustment is an obvious example, but there are others, including the economic protectionism of blocs like the EU. In addition, with the rise of global 'corporate' actors, nation states often see themselves as losing their traditional influence. This undoubtedly presents citizens with a challenge. It is important to continue lobbying for changes in world trade agreements, international debt policies and other such concerns. However, this action will be much more successful if it is accompanied by pressure on governments not to concede certain powers to influential transnational actors. Now more than ever the success of the politics of human rights depends on the determination of governments to regulate the industries that operate within their borders, to bring moral values to bear on the arms industry and to resist the gradual erosion of their ability to govern. The complex interaction between local and global politics and policies may mean that it is as citizens of our own states that we can most effectively bring the values of human rights to bear globally.

One of the most problematic aspects of the politics of human rights has been the issue of compliance. Not only has there been a significant gap between what many governments have signed up to and their actual practice, but there has also been a history of gross violation of human rights in many regions of the world. Events over the past three decades in Chile, South Africa, Rwanda, the Balkans and elsewhere have brought to the

---

4 See Mary Robinson's address at the Annual Global Ethic Lecture, University of Tübingen, Germany in January 2002, reported in the Irish Times January 21st 2002

fore, once again, the question of how the international community should deal with massive human rights tragedies, genocide and international acts of terrorism and aggression. This is not a new problem. However, questions concerning the aftermath of atrocities, whether these happen inside or across national boundaries, have increased both in frequency and complexity since the end of the Cold War. While there is consensus that, at a global level, a successful human rights culture requires effective accountability and compliance mechanisms, there are different perspectives on how best this can be realised.

This is a complex issue. On the one hand, there is a recognition that hard won gains in the field of human rights will continue to be undermined unless the international community puts mechanisms in place to end the culture of impunity enjoyed by many violators of human rights. On the other hand, the political survival of societies in transition from conflict or regimes where human rights violations were the norm may require settlements which prioritise the need for immediate social stability and peace over the need to bring to justice those who violated human rights. Some countries have succeeded in prosecuting the violators while also building new political institutions. Others have granted amnesty to those who committed particular crimes during a prior regime. The international community, aware of the serious difficulties created by this culture of impunity, established the International Criminal Tribunal for the Former Yugoslavia in 1993 and the following year set up the International Criminal Tribunal for Rwanda. Although each tribunal has had difficulties and the International Criminal Tribunal for Rwanda has had to be supplemented by more local forms of justice, these bodies have already had a significant impact on the seriousness with which human rights violations are now regarded. Moreover, with the coming into being of the International Criminal Court in July 2002, there is renewed hope that the world may be moving towards a new phase in the enforcement of human rights standards.

Alongside the growth of mechanisms for prosecuting perpetrators of human rights violations, there is another phenomenon that seeks to achieve reconciliation through truth in the wake of such violations. The most successful example of this is South Africa's Truth and Reconciliation Commission (TRC which has now finished much of its initial work. The TRC has provided amnesties for those perpetrators of human rights violations who have told the truth about their past and admitted their deeds to the victims. Some commentators have argued that offering an amnesty to these perpetrators and forgiving enemies has in fact denied justice to the victims. Others have pointed out that the TRC has embodied a different kind of justice, one that seeks to end the cycle by which each atrocity begets sill more atrocities. Thus, any need for punishment is subordinated to that of reconciliation through truth-telling. No doubt this is an imaginative and risky endevour. Moreover, inspired as it is by Christian ideas of forgiveness, it has as many detractors as it has supporters. Nonetheless, it suggests yet another mechanism by which the international community can hope to build a culture of compliance and adherence to human rights standards.

The language of human rights merits continued support. It enables us to attend to disparities in power relations, to the systemic exclusion of marginalised people on grounds of difference, to ideologies of domination and subordination and to discriminatory practices. The philosophy of human rights facilitates a scrutiny of the dynamics of relationships and directs us to a consideration of fundamental values and principles. In particular it focuses attention on the balance that must be reached between the interests of the individual and those of the wider community. And, although it does have its limitations, there is no other contender for its position as the global language for the advancement of human dignity and equality.